Reading/Writing Companion

Mc
Graw
Hill

mheducation.com/prek-12

Send all inquiries to:
McGraw Hill
1325 Avenue of the Americas
New York, NY 10019

ISBN: 978-1-26-573832-7
MHID: 1-26-573832-7

Printed in the United States of America.

3 4 5 6 7 8 9 LMN 26 25 24 23 22   A

Welcome to WONDERS!

We are so excited about how much you will learn and grow this year! We're here to help you set goals for your learning.

You will build on what you already know and learn new things every day.

You will read a lot of fun stories and interesting texts on different topics.

You will write about the texts you read. You will also write texts of your own. You will do research as well.

You will explore new ideas by reading different texts.

Each week, we will set goals on the My Goals page. Here is an example:

I can read and understand texts.

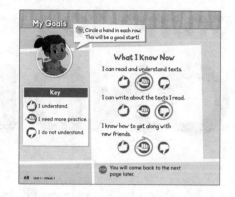

As you read and write, you will learn skills and strategies to help you reach your goals.

You will think about your learning and sometimes circle a hand to show your progress.

Here are some questions you can ask yourself.

- Did I understand the task?
- Was it easy?
- Was it hard?
- What made it hard?

It is okay if I need more practice. The most important thing is to do my best and keep learning!

If you need more help, you can choose what to do.

- Talk to a friend or teacher.
- Use an Anchor Chart.
- Choose a center activity.

At the end of each week, you will complete a fun task to show what you have learned.

Then you will return to your My Goals page and think about your learning.

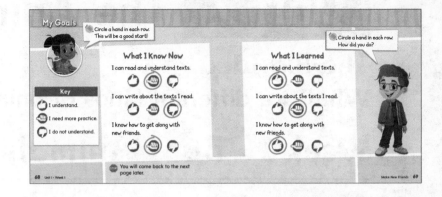

I learned so much about reading and understanding texts. I started with a sideways thumb, and now I circled the thumbs up for that goal!

Let's get started!

Unit 7 The Animal Kingdom

The Big Idea

Week 1 • Baby Animals

Digital Tools Find this eBook and other resources at: **my.mheducation.com**

Week 2 • Pet Pals

Week 3 • Animal Habitats

The Animal Kingdom

The Big Idea

What are different kinds of animals?

- -

 Talk about the different animals in the picture.

 Circle animals in the picture you have seen or read about.

 Describe another animal you know about.

Build Knowledge

Build Vocabulary

 Talk about how some animals are alike and different. What words tell about how they are alike and different?

 Draw a picture of one of the words.

 Write the word.

Image Source/Corbis

My Goals

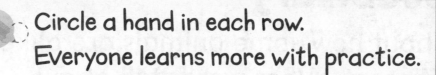 Circle a hand in each row.
Everyone learns more with practice.

What I Know Now

I can read and understand texts.

I can write about the texts I read.

I know how some animals are alike and different.

Key

 I understand.

 I need more practice.

 I do not understand.

 You will come back to the next page later.

Circle a hand in each row. What helped you the most?

What I Learned

I can read and understand texts.

I can write about the texts I read.

I know how some animals are alike and different.

Retell the nonfiction text.

 Write about the text.

One interesting fact I learned is

_____

- -

_____

- -

_____

Text Evidence

Page

One new baby animal name I learned is

 Text Evidence

- -

_____

Page

Talk about baby animals you know.

 Draw and **write** about your favorite baby animal.

My favorite baby animal is

Write a Sentence

  Talk about the baby animals in the text.

Listen to this sentence about baby animals.

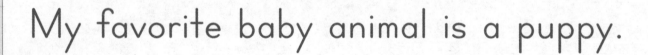

My favorite baby animal is a puppy.

 Circle the capital letter in the sentence.

Writing Skill

Remember: Every sentence begins with a capital letter.

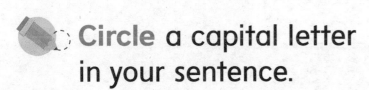

Write a sentence about your favorite baby animal.

_____

_____

_____

_____

Circle a capital letter
in your sentence.

A **fact** in a text is information about a topic that can be proven true or false. An **opinion** is a thought or feeling about a topic.

 Listen to and **look** at pages 14–15.

 Talk about the facts and opinions.

 Write one fact and one opinion.

One fact is

_____

- -

_____

_____

- -

_____

One opinion is

_____

- - - - - - - - - - - - - - - - - -

_____

- - - - - - - - - - - - - - - - - -

_____

_____

- - - - - - - - - - - - - - - - - -

_____

 Talk about which word helps you spot an opinion. Explain.

 Check In

 Look at the fennec fox on page 7.

 Talk about why the author and photographer include this photo.

 Write two facts you can learn about the fox from this photo.

The fennec fox has

_____

1. _____

_____

2. _____

Listen to and **look** at pages 28–29.

 Talk about why the author says the wombat's paws are like "built-in shovels."

 Draw and **write** about the wombat's paws.

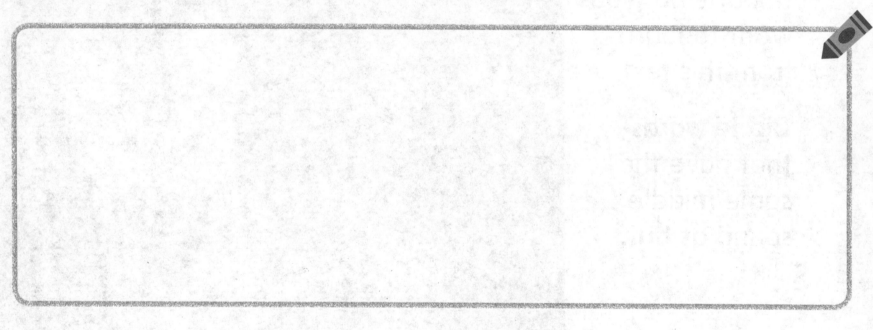

The wombat's paws

_____

- - - - - - - - - - - - - - - - - - - -

_____

A Pup and a Cub

Find Text Evidence

Read the title. Look at the photos. Think about what you want to learn from this text.

Circle words that have the same middle sound as **but**.

I am a pup.

I have a mom and a dad.

Find Text Evidence

 Underline and read the word **have**.

 Draw a box around the animal on page 23 that is not a pet.

I am in a pack.

We sit in a den.

I am not a pet.

I have not met a pet pup!

🔍 **Find Text Evidence**

✏️ **Circle** words that have the same middle sound as **mud**.

✏️ **Underline** words that tell where the cub on page 25 is.

I am a cub.

Mom and Dad see me.

I sit on a rock in the sun.

I nap in the sun a lot!

 **Find Text Evidence**

Circle words that begin with the same sound as **us**.

Retell the text. Reread if you do not understand something.

Sis and I have fun.

We can go up, up!

Aditya Singh/Moment Open/Getty Images

A pup can run for fun.

A cub can run for fun.

Oliver

Write About the Shared Read

A Pup and a Cub

How are the two lion cubs alike?

 Look at what Oliver drew.

 Listen to what he wrote.

Grammar

A **verb** tells what someone or something is doing.

StockImageFactory.com/Shutterstock

The lion cubs live with their mom and dad.

They both have brown fur.

Both of the little cubs climb up in the tree.

That is how they have fun!

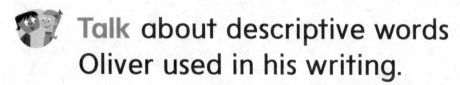 **Talk** about descriptive words Oliver used in his writing.

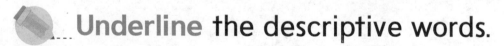 **Underline** the descriptive words.

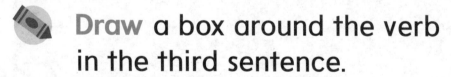 **Draw** a box around the verb in the third sentence.

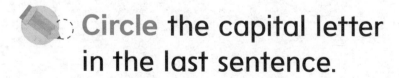 **Circle** the capital letter in the last sentence.

Writing Trait

Remember: Descriptive words make your writing more interesting.

Write About the Shared Read

A Pup
and a Cub

How are the wolf pup and lion cub alike?

 Talk about the question.

 Draw your ideas.

Write about your ideas.
Use your drawing to help you.

_____

- -

_____

- -

_____

_____

- -

_____

- -

_____

Remember:

☐ Add descriptive words.

☐ Use verbs.

☐ Capitalize the first word in every sentence.

Check In

Listen to "Over in the Meadow."
Which words in the poem rhyme?

 Draw the word that rhymes with *one*.

 Write the word.

The word that rhymes with *one* is

Listen to "Kitty Caught a Caterpillar."

 Circle the animals Kitty did catch.

 Draw a box around the animal that Kitty did not catch.

Animal Features

Step 1 Talk about animals and their special features. Choose one to learn about.

Step 2 Write a question about how your animal uses its special features.

_____

- -

_____

_____

- -

_____

Step 3 Look at books or use the Internet.
Look up words you do not know.
You can use a picture dictionary.

Step 4 **Draw** and **write** about what you learned.

Step 5 **Choose** a good way to present your work.

 Talk about these animals. How are they alike? How are they different?

 Compare these animals to the animals in *ZooBorns!*

Quick Tip

You can use these sentence starters:

The animals in the art ____.

The animals in ZooBorns! ____.

Make an Animal Puppet

① **Think** about the texts you read. What did you learn about how animals are alike and different?

② **Choose** a baby animal. **Make** a paper bag puppet of this animal. **Draw** what makes this animal special.

③ **Write** about what makes this animal special. Use words that you learned this week.

Think about what you learned this week.
Turn to page 11.

Build Knowledge

Build Vocabulary

 Talk about how to take care of different kinds of pets. What words tell about how to care for different pets?

 Draw a picture of one of the words.

Write the word.

_____

- -

_____

My Goals

 Circle a hand in each row.
It is important to keep learning.

Key

 I understand.

 I need more practice.

 I do not understand.

What I Know Now

I can read and understand texts.

I can write about the texts I read.

I know how to take care of different kinds of pets.

 You will come back to the next page later.

Circle a hand in each row. What is getting easier?

What I Learned

I can read and understand texts.

I can write about the texts I read.

I know how to take care of different kinds of pets.

Retell the realistic fiction story.

Write about the story.

Danny wants a turtle because

Text Evidence

Page

_____

- -

_____

This is realistic fiction because

_____

- -

_____

Text Evidence

Page

- -

_____

Talk about a pet you would like to get.

 Draw and **write** about why you would want this pet.

I would want this pet because

Write a Sentence

 Talk about what the story tells about caring for a pet.

 Listen to this sentence about caring for a pet.

> I feed my pet hamster celery.

 Draw an arrow below the sentence from the first word to the last word.

Writing Skill

Remember:
When you write, the words go from left to right.

Write a sentence about caring for a pet.

_____

- - - - - - - - - - - - - - - - - -

_____

- - - - - - - - - - - - - - - - - -

_____

- - - - - - - - - - - - - - - - - -

_____

 Draw an arrow below your sentence from the first word to the last word.

The important events in a story often have
a problem and a solution.

- **The problem** is what a character
  wants to do or fix.

- **The way the character solves the problem**
  is the solution.

 Listen carefully to part of the story.

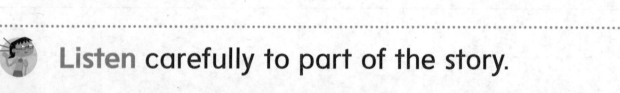 **Talk** and **write** about Danny's problem.

Draw and **write** about the solution.

The solution is

_____

- -

_____

Check In

Listen for rhyming words on pages 11–12. What word helps you predict Danny's next pet?

 Talk about how the two words are alike.

 Draw both words.

Listen to and **look** at pages 24–25.

 Talk about how Danny feels about the turtle.

 Draw and **write** about how he feels.

Danny feels

I Hug Gus!

 Read the title. Look at the pictures. Think about what you want to find out in this story.

 Circle words that end with the same sound as **tag**.

I can see a big, red pup.

I pick a pup for a pet.

🔍 **Find Text Evidence**

✏️ **Underline** and read the word **They**.

✏️ **Circle** who can run, run, and win!

My big pup and a cat tug.

They tug and have fun.

Gus is a big, red pup.

Gus can run, run, and win!

Shared Read

🔍 Find Text Evidence

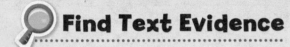 Underline and read the word of.

Circle two rhyming words.

Gus is on top of the bed.

He can sit up and beg.

Gus and I are on a rug.

Gus can tug, tug, tug!

Find Text Evidence

Circle words that begin with the same sound as **get**.

Retell the story in order. Use the words and pictures to help you with parts you do not understand.

I rub Gus in the tub.

Gus is wet, wet, wet!

I tuck Gus in a big bed.

I can hug, hug, hug Gus!

Luke

Write About the Shared Read

I Hug Gus!

What if you got a new pet? Write a story about when you got a new pet.

 Look at what Luke drew.

 Listen to what he wrote.

Grammar

A **past-tense verb** tells about actions that already happened.

Andersen Ross/Blend Images/Getty Images

My mom said I could get a pet.

So we walked to the animal shelter.

An orange cat in a cage looked at me.

I knew he was the best pet for me!

 Talk about descriptive words Luke used in his writing.

 Circle the descriptive words.

 Underline the past-tense verbs in the second and third sentences.

 Draw an arrow below the first sentence from the first word to the last word.

Writing Trait

Remember: Descriptive words make your writing more interesting.

Write About the Shared Read

I Hug Gus!

What would your first day with a new pet have been like? Write a story about it.

 Talk about the question.

 Draw your ideas.

Write about your ideas.
Use your drawing to help you.

_____

- - - - - - - - - - - - - - - - -

_____

- - - - - - - - - - - - - - - - -

_____

- - - - - - - - - - - - - - - - -

_____

- - - - - - - - - - - - - - - - -

_____

Remember:

☐ Add descriptive words.

☐ Use past-tense verbs.

☐ Write from left to right.

Check In

Listen to the personal narrative.

 Circle the character who is telling the story. Write her name.

 Talk about words that help you know the author is telling the story about herself.

Quick Tip

You can use these sentence starters:

The character telling the story is ____.

The author is ____.

Listen to pages 34–35. How does Lola use sound words to make her story come to life?

 Draw and **write** about Bella making a sound.

Write About It

Lola wrote about herself and a pet. Now write a personal narrative about yourself and a pet you have or know. Include sound words.

A sound Bella makes is

Caring for a Pet

Step 1 **Talk** about how you would care for different pets. Choose one pet to learn about.

Step 2 **Write** a question about how to care for this pet.

_____

- -

_____

- -

_____

Step 3 **Look** at books or use the Internet. Look up words you do not know. You can use a picture dictionary.

Step 4 Draw what you learned.

Step 5 Write about what you learned
in your writer's notebook.
Use new words that you learned.

Step 6 Choose a good way to present your work.

Talk about the photo.
What clues tell you how this girl
feels about her pet rabbit?

 Compare this girl and her rabbit
to Danny and his turtle
in *The Birthday Pet*.

Quick Tip

You can use these
sentence starters:

The girl looks ____.

The rabbit looks ____.

Claudia Rehm, Red Chopsticks Images/Westend61/Getty Images

Write Pet Instructions

1 Think about the texts you read. What did you learn about how to take care of different kinds of pets?

2 Choose an animal that might live at an animal shelter. What kind of care does this animal need?

3 Draw and **write** instructions for a new pet owner. Explain how to take care of this pet. Use words that you learned this week.

Think about what you learned this week. Turn to page 41.

Build Knowledge

? Essential Question **Where do animals live?**

Build Vocabulary

 Talk about where animals live.
What are some words that name
places where animals live?

 Draw a picture of one of the places.

 Write the word.

My Goals

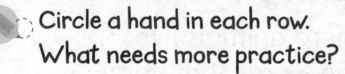 Circle a hand in each row.
What needs more practice?

Key

 I understand.

 I need more practice.

 I do not understand.

What I Know Now

I can read and understand texts.

I can write about the texts I read.

I know where animals live.

 You will come back to the next page later.

Circle a hand in each row. Great job!

What I Learned

I can read and understand texts.

I can write about the texts I read.

I know where animals live.

Retell the fantasy story.

Write about the fantasy.

Bear Snores On

In Bear's den, the animals

Text Evidence

Page

I know this is a fantasy because

Text Evidence

Page

Talk about what real animals do in the winter.

 Draw and **write** about a real animal in the winter.

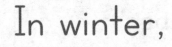

In winter,

_____

- -

_____

Write a Sentence

 Talk about the bear in the story.

 Listen to this sentence about bears.

> Bears sleep during the winter.

 Circle the Word Bank word *the*.

Writing Skill

Remember:
You can use your
Word Bank to help
you spell words.

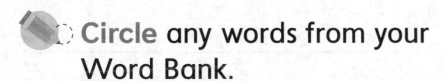

Write a sentence about something you do in winter.

_____

- -

_____

_____

- -

_____

_____

- -

_____

Circle any words from your Word Bank.

A **cause** is what makes an **event** happen in a story. An **effect** is the event that happens.

 Listen to and **look** at pages 8–9.

 Talk about what causes Mouse to go in the cave.

 Write about the cause and effect.

The weather is

_____

_____

This causes Mouse to

_____

_____

Listen to and **look** at pages 24–26.
What causes Bear to wake up?

 Draw the cause and effect.

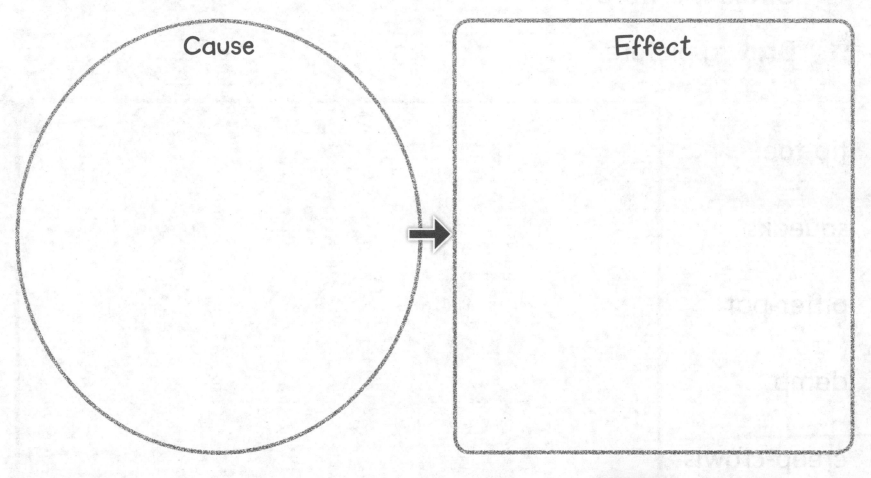

Cause

Effect

Listen to and **look** at pages 8–9.
The events begin in a quiet way.
Which words help you picture this?

 Circle the words.

 Draw a picture.

tip-toe

squeaks

pitter-pat

damp

creep-crawls

Listen to and **look** at pages 32–34.

 Talk about the end of the story. Why do you think the author ends the story this way?

 Draw and **write** about it.

At the end of the story,

_____

- -

_____

Find Text Evidence

Make a prediction about the story. Use the title and pictures to help you. Read to find out if your prediction is correct.

Circle words that begin with the same sound as **vat**.

A Vet in a Van

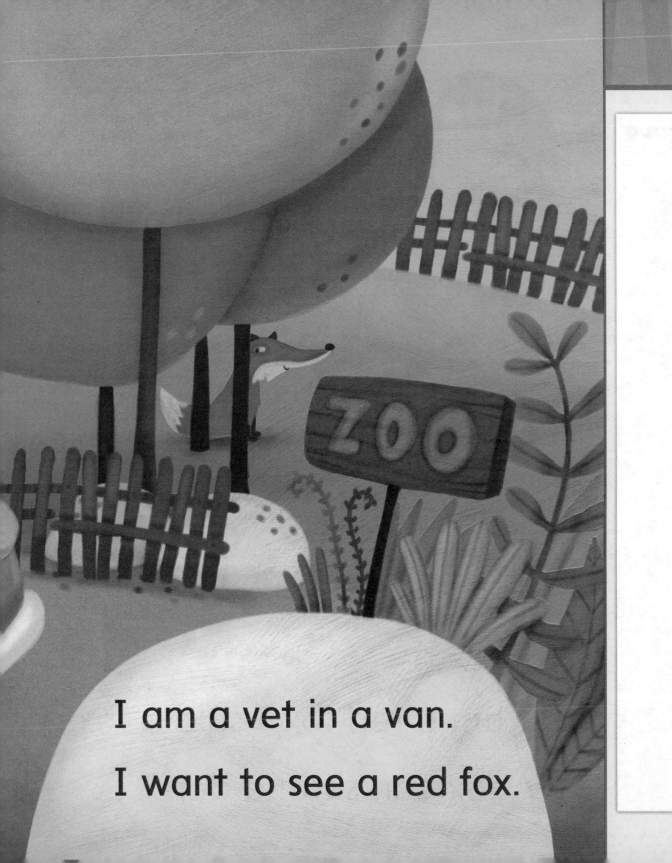

I am a vet in a van.

I want to see a red fox.

Shared Read

🔍 **Find Text Evidence**

✏️ <u>Underline</u> and read the words **said** and **want**.

✏️ **Circle** who the vet wants to see on page 83.

"I am a red fox," said a fox.

"A fox can sit in a den."

I want to see a big cat.

I can go in my van.

Find Text Evidence

Think about what has happened so far. Make a prediction about what will happen next.

Circle the picture that shows six pigs.

"I am a big cat," said a cat.

"I can sit on a rock."

I can see a pig.

I can see six!

Shared Read

 Find Text Evidence

Circle words that end with the same sounds as **box**.

Talk about your prediction. Was it correct? Use the words and pictures to help you decide. Then retell the story.

I see a sick ox.

I can fix a bad leg.

"I met a vet!" said the ox.

"A vet can fix a sick ox!"

Nikki

Write About the Shared Read

Pretend you are the vet in the story.
What will you like doing?
Write your opinion.

 Look at what Nikki drew.

 Listen to what she wrote.

A Vet in a Van

Grammar

A **future-tense verb** tells about actions that will happen in the future.

Africa Studio/Shutterstock

I will like helping the fox.

I like its long, funny nose.

I will help the ox, too.

He will look cute with the bandage on.

 Talk about descriptive words Nikki used in her writing.

 Underline two descriptive words in the second sentence.

 Draw boxes around the future-tense verbs in the first and last sentences.

 Circle the Word Bank word *with* in the last sentence.

Writing Trait

Remember: Descriptive words make your writing more interesting.

Write About the Shared Read

Will you be a vet when you grow up?
Why or why not? Write your opinion.

 Talk about the question.

 Draw your ideas.

Write about your ideas.
Use your drawing to help you.

_____

_____

_____

_____

_____

_____

_____

Check In

Look at the animal habitats.
How are they alike and different?

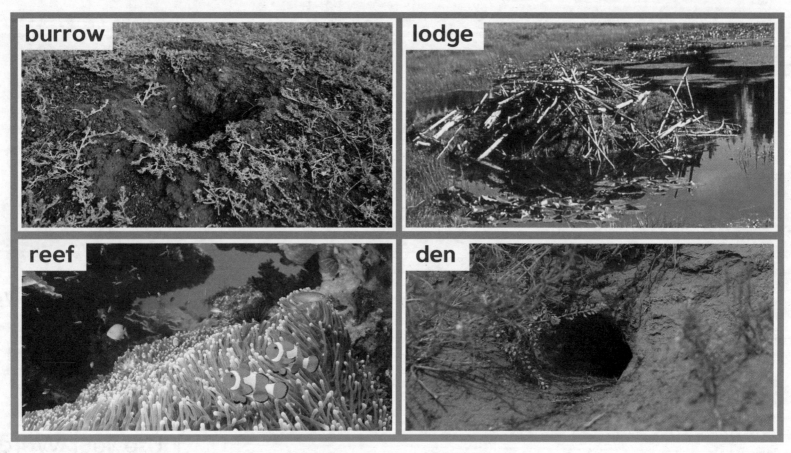

burrow

lodge

reef

den

 Circle the animal habitats
that are underground.

 Draw boxes around the habitats
that are in the water.

Look at page 38. What does the author want you to know?

 Write about it.

The small picture shows

The label tells

The photo shows

Quick Tip

To talk about animal habitats, you can say:

This animal lives in a ___.

It is a good habitat because ___.

Talk About It

Look at pages 38–39. The beaver and the clown fish both live in the water. How are their habitats alike and different?

Animal Habitats

Step 1 **Talk** about animal habitats.
Choose one to learn about.

Step 2 **Write** a question about the habitat.

_____

- -

_____

_____

- -

_____

Step 3 **Look** at books or use the Internet.
Look up words you do not know.
You can use a picture dictionary.

Step 4 Draw what you learned.

Step 5 Write about what you learned in your writer's notebook. Use new words that you learned.

Step 6 Choose a good way to present your work.

A meerkat mother and pup look out of their burrow.

 Talk about the photo.

 Compare the meerkat habitat with Bear's habitat in *Bear Snores On.*

Quick Tip

You can use these sentence starters:

The meerkat habitat is ____.

Bear's habitat is ____.

Write About a Habitat

1 **Think** about the texts you read. What did you learn about where animals live?

2 **Choose** an animal. **Draw** the animal in its habitat.

3 **Write** about how the habitat helps the animal. Use words that you learned this week.

Think about what you learned this week.
Turn to page 71.

Think About Your Learning

Think about what you learned in this unit.

 Share one thing you did well.

 Write one thing you want to get better at.

_____

- - - - - - - - - - - - - - - - - - -

_____

- - - - - - - - - - - - - - - - - - -

_____

Share a goal you have with your partner.

My Sound-Spellings

Aa — a — apple	Bb — b — bat	Cc — c ck k — camel	Dd — d — dolphin	Ee — e — egg	Ff — f — fire	Gg — g — guitar
Hh — h_ — hippo	Ii — i — insect	Jj — j — jump	Kk — c k ck — koala	Ll — l — lemon	Mm — m — map	Nn — n — nest
Oo — o — octopus	Pp — p — piano	Qq — qu_ — queen	Rr — r — rose	Ss — s — sun	Tt — t — turtle	Uu — u — umbrella
Vv — v — volcano	Ww — w_ — window	Xx — x — box	Yy — y_ — yo-yo	Zz — z _s — zipper		

Handwriting Models

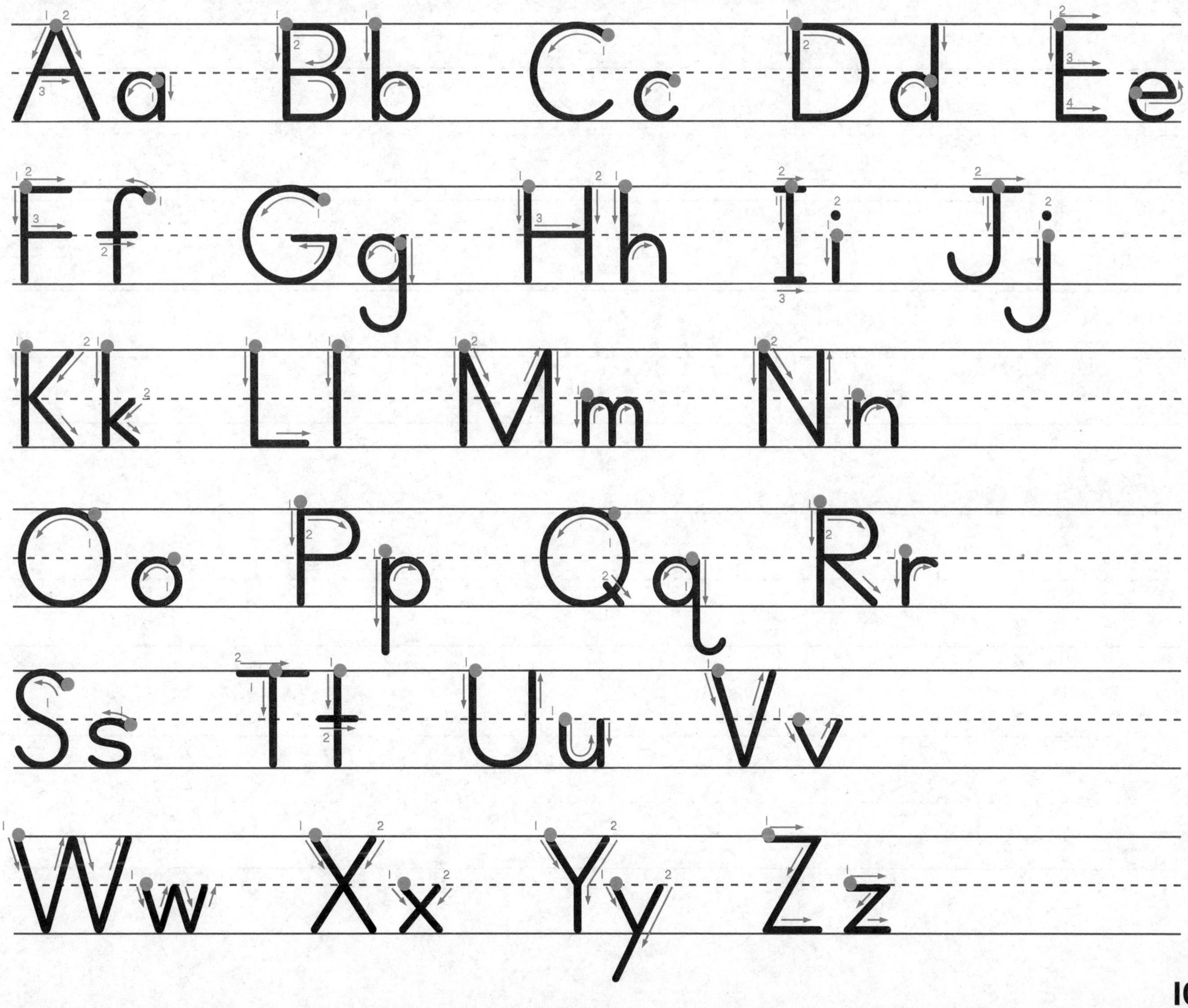

Aa Bb Cc Dd Ee
Ff Gg Hh Ii Jj
Kk Ll Mm Nn
Oo Pp Qq Rr
Ss Tt Uu Vv
Ww Xx Yy Zz